DIVERSITY IN HIGHER EDUCATION: REFORM IN THE COLLEGES

By Ronald Gross

Library of Congress Catalog Card Number: 75-39100
ISBN 0-87367-069-8
Copyright © 1976 by The Phi Delta Kappa Educational Foundation
Bloomington, Indiana

TABLE OF CONTENTS

Reforms in Higher Education 6
    Individualization 9
    New Role for the Teacher 10
    The Learning Contract 10
    The Planning Portfolio 11
    Wide-Ranging Resources for Learning 13
    Providing Alternatives and Options 15

Implications for the Schools 20

Selected Bibliography 24

LB
2341
.675

Acknowledgments

The material from Empire State College on p. 11 is adapted from the College's 1972 Bulletin with permission of the College.

The material cited from *Guide to Alternative Colleges and Universities* on p. 16 is reprinted by permission of Beacon Press. Copyright © 1974 by Wayne Blaze, Bill Hertzberg, and Roy Krantz.

The material about the Human Relations Work-Study Center on p. 18 is preprinted from an article to appear in *Parents' Magazine*.

REFORMS IN HIGHER EDUCATION

Nicholas France recently received his college diploma at the age of 27—without ever having gone to college. He studied on his own, passed an examination that proved he knew as much as a college graduate, and received a degree.

He is the first such graduate in the country, but many others may soon join him, if programs like this catch on throughout the United States.

France, who is married and the father of a two-year-old son, lives in a suburb of New York City. While serving in the Army in 1965 he took the United States Armed Forces Institute college-equivalency exams, a five-hour battery of tests. His good marks on those tests earned him three semesters of college credit.

After returning to New York City, France started working with the U.S. Treasury Department's Bank Examiner's office in New York as a financial intern, learning banking and accounting on the job. One day he saw a poster advertising the Regents External Degree Program on a library bulletin board.

By paying $10 he was enrolled in the business administration program. He received a couple of 40-page mimeographed study guides, purchased about twenty books, and studied on his own for about two years.

When he was ready in September, 1974, France took the eleven-hour set of exams that New York state requires of candidates for the degree. He made it. Total cost for his college education: about $410.

"We figure he knows just about as much as the graduate of a

traditional college," says Robert Anstett, registrar of the program. "That's what the exam's designed to test."

"I had a little trouble with the Treasury Department," France said, "when I told them I'd soon have my degree through this method. They asked if it was a correspondence course, which they won't accept. But when I told them that the State of New York would certify the degree, they said it was O.K."

On the basis of earning his degree, France has been promoted from financial intern to assistant national bank examiner and received a $2,000 raise.

"I could never have managed to go back to a regular college," says France. "With a wife and child and a full-time job, I would have been behind the eight-ball for the rest of my life for lack of that diploma. This kind of program gives people like me a second chance for success."

Mr. France is currently pursuing a master's degree at Ionia College in his spare time.

Nicholas France is a product of a new pattern of teaching and learning that has emerged strongly in higher education in the past five years. This pattern simultaneously derives from open education in elementary and secondary schools and may soon impinge on the reform movement there.

Variously known as Open Learning, Nontraditional Study, the External Degree, and the Extended (or Expanded) Campus, this movement contains the most promising impulses toward humanization, flexibility, and individualization.

Literally hundreds of colleges and universities throughout the country are currently experimenting with such programs, and even more have them on the drawing boards. At a time when most colleges are cutting back, this is one area that is expanding.

The movement in higher education is already so widespread that there is no way to keep track of its proliferation. A recently published directory, which was highly selective, listed 250 programs, which would represent one of every ten institutions in the nation. Based on the best available estimates from the Office of New Degree Programs set up by the College Entrance Examination Board and the Educational Testing Service to monitor these initiatives, and on my own visits to representative campuses around the country, I would estimate that between one-quarter and one-half of all colleges are now offering at least one major "alternative" program for undergraduates or a "nontraditional" degree program for older students or both.

Some of the programs have been operating for years and have thus become nationally known, such as those of Goddard College, Syracuse University, the New School for Social Research in New York City, and the University of Oklahoma. In other cases new institutions have been created to offer new options for learners. In this category the leading examples are Empire State College (New York), Thomas Edison College (New Jersey), Campus-Free College (Boston), and the University of Mid-America (Nebraska).

Nationally, the most notable development is the University Without Walls, which has "units" at campuses scattered across the country. These programs, which differ considerably from one campus to another, share the concept that each student's program should be derived from his or her own needs and goals and should use a wide range of learning resources and experiences rather than relying solely or mainly on classroom instruction.

In addition to these B.A. programs, of course, a number of "open" or "external" graduate degree programs exist, such as those in the field of education offered by Nova University, the University of Massachusetts, and the Union Graduate School.

Along with other factors, these programs indicate self-interest of the colleges, which are finding it increasingly difficult to purvey the same programs to the same people. On one hand, they are running out of young people to teach, since the birth rate is declining. They have seen the panic caused in elementary schools by this phenomenon and are reaching out for a new constituency to keep seats filled. They have noted, too, that young people who are going to college often want something different from the conventional fare. So the values of open education have begun to manifest themselves on campus. This is important for all of us in the schools for several reasons.

First, it shows that the principles that have proved potent in the best elementary and secondary classrooms are equally valid for higher education and for learning throughout life, thus lending them additional authority and suggesting that schools may be preparing children well for later learning.

Second, changes in pedagogical styles on campuses mean that students coming from open learning programs in elementary and secondary schools will find a more congenial setting, and a readier welcome, in colleges.

Finally, since the educational values of higher education have always exerted formidable pressure, whether good or evil, on secondary schools, it should be salutary to have more models in universities of open institutions, programs, and classrooms.

What are the values that are increasingly common to open education in both the schools and colleges? Among them are individualization, new roles for the teacher, wide-ranging resources for learning, and a variety of options.

Individualization

The keynote definition of nontraditional study was provided by the Commission on Nontraditional Study sponsored by the College Entrance Examination Board and Educational Testing Service. The commission had the same trouble defining its subject as a group of teachers would have defining open education and ended up characterizing it as an "attitude" rather than a specific program. But this "attitude" is bold and radical. It proclaims the primacy of the learner, while being kindly hospitable to a wide variety of institutional and individual styles:

> It is an attitude that puts the student first and the institution second, concentrates more on the former's need than the latter's convenience, encourages diversity of individual opportunity, and deemphasizes time and space or even course requirements in favor of competence and, where applicable, performance. It is not a new attitude; it is simply a more prevalent one than before. It has concern for the learner of any age and circumstances, for the degree aspirant or the person who finds a sufficient reward in enriching life through constant, periodic, or occasional study. It is an attitude that can stimulate exciting and high quality educational progress.

Obviously, this "attitude"—in its affirmation of the individual's importance, its egalitarian "inviting in" of everyone to a sector of education formerly reserved for the "qualified," and its emphasis on diversity and options—is one that dominates our ideals in schools. Needless to say, American higher education is far from realizing these ideals in practice. But it is important, and new, for those in power to affirm such aspirations.

New Role for the Teacher

As in open classrooms or new-style high schools, the new program in higher education offers new roles for teachers. The traditional role of the college professor as lecturer, dispenser of information, seminar leader, and quiz-giver is changing to a more sophisticated posture. Variously called a "mentor," "advisor," "consultant," or "facilitator," the teacher in this new role is not primarily a conveyor of information to groups of students. Rather, the professor will work intensively with individual students, helping each one to figure out, articulate, and plan what, why, how, where, and when he or she can learn best.

Obviously, such a role requires capacities quite different from the lecturing and testing of traditional college teaching. In conventional classroom teaching, a professor might go through an entire career without developing a really intimate, personal relationship with an individual student. But for a mentor, such eyeball-to-eyeball discussion is a daily occurrence. Under the traditional system, the teacher imposed demands and made key decisions about what was worth learning and how it would be learned. In the new approach, decision making is shared.

The Learning Contract

But how can a student's higher education actually be shaped around his or her unique characteristics as a person? The learning contract, which was pioneered in the schools years ago, is the basic medium for this kind of education. It "specifies the learning activities to be undertaken, the duration of the study, the criteria by which the work is to be evaluated, and the amount of credit to be assigned," says one expert practitioner, Nancy Avakian of Empire State College. "The contract addresses itself to various dimensions of learning: the long-range plans of the student, specific purposes or topics, the learning activities to be undertaken, and the means and criteria of evaluation."

Under such a system, a student and a mentor devise an individualized program of study based on the student's personal goals and ambitions. Then learning proceeds through a series of contracts negotiated between the learner and the mentor, who represents the institution. "These programs often stress individualized and flexible programs of learning," says Samuel Baskin, director of the University Without Walls. "They may include various strategies of learning—classrooms, work experience, internship, technological aids, learning contracts, travel, self-directed study, and research—that might best suit the achievement of the student's learning goals."

Here is a description of the planning portfolio every entering student prepares in a typical open college:

THE PLANNING PORTFOLIO

At the end of the initial seminar each student will have assembled the materials for a planning portfolio, which will be a basic working tool for the remainder of his/her study. The portfolio will be constantly referred to as a checkpoint for evaluating a student's progress and as a framework for planning. The material in the portfolio is subject to revision as the student continues to grow educationally.

Documents in the initial portfolio will include:

a summary of all previous postsecondary work
a paper on educational philosophy
a narrative statement of individual goals
a narrative statement assessing the individual's abilities
a long-range planning form
a one-year planning form

All future learning contracts and records of all planning and evaluation sessions will be added to the portfolio. As the learning experiences are completed, any materials produced will also become part of the student's file.

On the basis of such documentation, an individual program leading to a degree can be negotiated with each student, usually through a number of successive "contracts." Such negotiations and resulting contracts usually focus on four areas. First, the student is helped to articulate long-range goals, both for life and for formal education. Then, within the context of these large goals, precise purposes are formulated for the next immediate segment of education: a year, a term, sometimes just for the next month. Third, specific activities and resources for learning are inventoried, researched if necessary, and selected. Such resources may include independent study, work internships, formal course work, travel-as-learning, research, a cooperative effort with others, or learning from a tutor. Finally, the student and the advisor work out a sound way of evaluating and demonstrating the learning that has taken place and come to an agreement on the amount of credit (if they are working within that kind of system) to be awarded toward the degree.

The following student careers from Empire State College indicate the flexibility afforded by this approach at its best.

Sean Haskins, a 17-year-old high school student who has been accepted into Empire State College under early admissions, is working for a B.A. in history and will enter law school after graduation. He is also interested in economics and political science.

Sean's first contract is full time for three summer months. The contract is in three parts; these are chosen according to Sean's interests and are intended to broaden these interests as well as to remediate areas of deficiency.

The first part of the contract covers political literature. After reading Malraux, *Man's Fate,* Sean will write an analysis of the main character's personality and motivation. An examination of the role of the Party will follow a reading of Sartre, *Dirty Hands.* Solzhenitsyn's *The First Circle* will be scrutinized for what it means to say that a writer can be an alternative government. Similar analysis will be written based upon Sigal, *Weekend in Dimlock;* Heller, *Catch-22;* Orwell, "Shooting an Elephant"; and Brecht, *Mother Courage.* This section of the contract will be completed by viewing a videotape interview with Leslie Fiedler, in which he discusses American literature and raises the question of the political responsibilities of the creative writer.

The second part of the contract covers readings in social theory: Freud, *Introductory Lectures in Psychoanalysis;* Wilson, *To the Finland Station;* Marx, *The Communist Manifesto;* Veblen, *Theory of the Leisure Class;* Ellul, *Technological Society;* and Brown, *Love's Body.* The final exercise is to view a videotape interview of Albert Schwartz, who discusses psychohistory. Following this, Sean will be required to define some of the specialized vocabulary of the thinkers whose works he has read and to analyze Schwartz's discussion of Brown.

American history is studied in the third segment of the contract. Sean will read Morgan, *The Puritan Dilemma;* Miller, "The Marrow of Puritan Theology;" and Baritz, "John Winthrop: Political Theology." After viewing a videotape interview of Harry Harootunian, an expert on Asian studies, Sean will write a short paper on the advantages and disadvantages of comparative history.

Sean's final requirement in this contract is to write a paper on what he considers to be the major ingredients in the Puritan's formal theological world-view.

Dolores Guion has earned the equivalent of more than 200 college credits from institutions in the United States and abroad. An R.N., she is also coordinator for Health Occupations at a vocational center where she has been teaching and developing a curriculum to train nurses' aides to be L.P.N.'s. Mrs. Guion's ultimate goal is to direct a private school for practical nurses.

In her first contract with the college, she will begin a research field project with the assistance of specialists in the New York State Department of Health. She will examine institutions that train health service professionals to determine their educational effectiveness.

In addition, she will begin to develop a curriculum for the education of L.P.N.'s in high school. Her own job will furnish excellent access to planning and resource materials, people, and organizations.

Mrs. Guion will present a weekly log of her institutional research activities and a monthly record of her major research to her colleagues and her mentor. Her observations and preliminary conclusions will also be presented in a paper or an interdisciplinary seminar of faculty and students.

Wide-Ranging Resources for Learning

Higher education has carried the development of a wider range of resources even further than elementary and secondary schools have. Programs of study can now be built around the personal life-situation of each student, turning many ongoing experiences to educational use: work, hobbies, volunteer work, experiences in the family. A wide range of media and technologies is also being harnessed. For example, the University of Mid-America, a public consortium covering four states, offers college courses and employs a marvelous mix of media to reach students in every way possible. Courses are broadcast on television but are also available at libraries on videocassettes for playing by individual students who miss lessons. A WATS-line gives students in remote areas access to professors by phone. Newspapers carry course materials. Lessons are submitted and commented on through the mail. Radio carries announcements of changes in scheduling. Computers are currently being harnessed to serve students better. And, of course, a full range of printed materials, from traditional books to programmed texts, is placed in students' hands.

Using the students' own life-situations for educational purposes carries the process even further. Here are some profiles of how students and advisors in one open-learning institution, Washington (D.C.) International College, fit serious learning into the students' life and learn from a variety of sources and resources:

After a year of general study in a variety of areas, Sandi has decided to focus on art, mythology, and psychology. While recognizing that they may have great correlation between them, she also wants to do detailed, in-depth study in each area. Thus she has shaped a curriculum around a long-range learning experience in which she will attempt to integrate and synthesize her work in each area. Her major time commitment, however, is to explore aspects of these areas in depth—major schools of thought in psychology, the work of Abraham Maslow, two- and three-dimensional design, beginning general semantics. As a way of demonstrating skill competence, she will prepare a major project in several media summarizing her work.

Charles, an older student employed by the government, hopes to develop skill in organizing minority federal employees into a group. To accomplish this objective, he has planned a 15-credit internship in which he continues his activities with advice and assistance from a faculty advisor who is an expert in organization and management. In addition, Charles is pursuing specific study through tutorials in economics and other related areas.

When Karen enrolled at WIC, she had more than two years of previous college experience. However, she was interested in investigating a career in social work. After having an internship with the duties of a social worker, her career hopes were confirmed. A planning seminar with other students helped her design the rest of her undergraduate program and informed her of the variety of resources and learning modes available. Focusing studies on her goal, Karen has completed several seminars and tutorials, doing much reading in sociology and psychology. Community learning centers such as Washington School of Psychiatry and Philanthropon House have added to her learning experiences. Her undergraduate education has also included study in mathematics and photography.

Providing Alternatives and Options

In a sense, this whole movement in higher education is an attempt to create alternatives and options for students, as Mario Fantini and others have proposed. Until now, the path to a degree has been pretty narrow: to get on it, you had to be 18 to 22 years old, able to submit to a residency at a campus for several years, willing to pursue one of the preset programs available, and capable of learning from the few modes of instruction available in college classrooms.

Fifteen years ago, as David Riesman and Christopher Jencks pointed out, virtually every college in the country secretly aspired to become as much like Harvard or Columbia as it could. Community colleges aspired to become four-year colleges as quickly as possible, four-year institutions wanted to become mini-universities, and so on. With only one model of excellence, little freedom existed for an institution to pursue an alternate goal with quite different students—and win distinction for its success.

The alternatives movement in higher education endeavors to provide other options. It seeks to facilitate higher learning for people of all ages and conditions of life, relevant to their highly individual goals and aspirations and according to their requirements and constraints.

On an increasing proportion of college campuses, students are finding a variety of options through which they can make their educational experience more flexible and varied. The range and character of these options are suggested succinctly by the *Guide to Alternative Colleges and Universities*, which identifies these alternative methods of delivering higher education:

Independent study is individual research or study that is conceived and carried out by the student with a faculty consultant and evaluator.

Directed study is similar to independent study because a student engages in some type of individual study or research. However, the two differ since faculty generally determine the curriculum and research design for the student.

Tutorials are similar to directed study but may include as many as four or five students, each receiving somewhat individualized attention. Tutorials often combine features of both independent study and directed study.

Experiential learning is a practical participatory experience bearing some relationship to a student's academic interests. A number of experiential learning models are employed by schools, all closely related and some differing in name only.

Field work, practicum, and *outreach* all refer to some type of practical participatory experience, either on or off campus. *Field term* is generally used to define field-work experiences that require a student's full participation for a semester. Usually no other course work is taken during the term.

Internships, apprenticeships, and *on the job training* are often field-work experiences supervised by both a faculty member and an outside resource person who is recognized as competent in the area.

Some schools use a *co-op program* (sometimes referred to as work-study), in which students are expected to locate and work in jobs relevant to their interests. Some co-op programs require a student to attend classes and work within a co-op placement simultaneously; others allow a student to alternate co-op quarters and on-campus quarters. In general, students do not receive academic credit for co-op experiences, though participation in the program is required for graduation. To offset academic costs, most students locate paying jobs.

Finally, a widely used method includes *foreign study, year abroad,* or *overseas programs.* Basically, students spend one year in a foreign country, usually the junior year, studying either at a foreign institution or in a special program set up by the student's parent institution. Many schools are beginning to design variations on this basic model, some permitting students to go abroad at any time, others extending the amount of time allowed overseas to two years, and so on.

The scope of the open-learning movement in higher education is best conveyed by briefly describing some representative programs and projects that illustrate the variety available.

One kind of "openness" uses technology to break the space-time constraints of classroom learning. Chicago's TV College, for example, has enabled hundreds of people to take college courses and earn a degree, if they wish, in their own living rooms. In a national application of the same principle, about 25,000 people enrolled in a course developed around Jacob Brownoski's unparalleled "The Ascent of Man," getting credit through 250 cooperating colleges and universities. Britain's Open University also illustrates this basic strategy of using technology to broaden access to higher learning, as well as to create more potent instructional presentations.

The way using technology can "open" the system to a wide range of learners is well stated by President D. B. Varner of the University of Mid-America. Looking toward rapidly developing communications technologies that can be harnessed to instructional uses, he writes, "Through television and audio-tapes and video-discs, the computer terminal, the newspaper, the textbook, and the study guide, (we shall be able) to make higher education available to the people of this country—all the people—on their own terms."

A second major kind of open higher learning aims to recognize that learning can take place without teaching—that people can and do learn all the time, and that such learning is just as legitimate as what is formally taught on campus. In response, various programs of validation and certification of learning have been developed. Through these, a learner may present experience and what has been learned from it, either by taking an examination or by presenting evidence in a portfolio to be evaluated. In more than 150 colleges "life experiences" ranging from Peace Corps service to community volunteer activities or running one's own business can now qualify for credit towards a degree.

For example, Roy Wagner, in his late thirties, came to Fordham University seeking training and a credential for counseling. He documented various experiences since high school, including studying for several years in a Franciscan seminary; spending time in the Army in Japan, studying the Japanese social system; and learning about issues in criminal justice as a New York City policeman. A faculty evaluation committee concluded after studying his records that Wagner's life experiences were worth 30 of the 128 credits necessary for the B.A. degree, which he completed three years later.

Outstanding examples of this form of open higher learning are New Jersey's Thomas Edison College and New York State's External Degree Program, through which students can obtain a B.A. or B.S. degree simply by passing the requisite examinations.

A third general category of options in higher learning might be described as learner-centered; this was discussed earlier. Perhaps the best-known institution with this approach is the University Without Walls. Other major examples are Minnesota Metropolitan College and the private Campus-Free College in Boston.

A fourth kind of open learning program focuses on broadening the standard college curriculum. People's learning needs alter greatly as they age and have mastered basic skills and common knowledge that schools try to impart to everyone. "The adult needs are perceived as different, and the adult potential for learning is seen as different," says John Valley, whose Office of New Degree Programs monitors initiatives in higher education. He notes that special needs of adult learners may be approached through special interdisciplinary courses instead of conventional college offerings. Or, he says, "The stress may be on stating degree requirements in various competencies instead of course units. The student is entitled to a degree whenever competency in all areas represented by the degree can be demonstrated."

An interesting example blending these two approaches is the long successful Human Relations Work-Study Program at the New School for Social Research in New York City, designed especially for women but exemplifying principles applicable to all mature learners.

The courses aren't the usual college fare of academic subjects arranged in strict hierarchies: English 101, Shakespeare, or Victorian Novelists. Rather, the curriculum is organized around skills and understandings that today's women need.

For instance, one large division centers on self-appraisal. Subjects include On Risking Change, New Ways of Being, Alone and Female, and Human Sexuality. Another group of courses revolves around communications skills; it includes offerings such as Talking with People, Public Speaking for Private People, and Writing as a Means of Self-Discovery.

Even more traditional courses in humanities and social sciences are presented with unusual twists. This term, for example, students could take The Present and Future of Women, An Encounter with Death, Parapsychology, or Sexual Politics in Modern Asia.

A course that is even more unconventional focuses on "learning by doing in community service." Here students get intensive experiences with professionals in fields such as family law, mental health, or nutrition.

All these courses are open to anyone who's interested—even men, though most of the students are women. A student who wants to pursue a cumulative program leading to a certificate puts together ten courses; at two or three courses a term, the certificate program takes from two to three years. To earn the certificate, a student must conclude her studies with an action project. "The outcome of learning should be action," says Ruth van Doren, the center's ebullient director. "You should be learning to do something, to produce some change in yourself or others or the world."

The center practices what it preaches, unlike a good many educational institutions that talk loftily but put students through a bureaucratic wringer. Certificates are awarded not on the basis of simply amassing credits for courses taken but for specific accomplishments that demonstrate what a student has learned to do. At this year's graduation exercises, which featured a poetry reading, musical performances, and everyone dancing together, students received certificates for such individual accomplishments as strengthening enforcement of local school bus regulations, being a volunteer art therapist at the Jewish Guild for Blind, researching the fear of hospitalization among mental patients, surveying the use of marijuana in a suburban community, conducting a series of self-awareness workshops for fellow black Americans in a ghetto community, founding a state association of administrative employees in religious institutions, and organizing art classes for widows through a social service agency.

IMPLICATIONS FOR THE SCHOOLS

What are the implications for schools of this growing tide of change on campuses? Several strong ones seem promising for the movement toward openness in schools. They make more defensible an individualized, flexible, option-filled program for students in elementary and secondary schools.

The most obvious implication is that more options and possibilities exist for students graduating from open high school programs. With most campuses developing alternatives for entering freshmen, including some that feature greater self-determination by the student, high school graduates who like this style of learning and have shown their competence in it have places to fit in—and can be welcomed more readily on the campuses.

A fairly typical option of this kind is "Unit One" at the University of Illinois. Open to freshmen and sophomores, the program can accept no more than 180 students a year and turns away about a third of the applicants. Unit One doesn't alter the regulations of the university; it supplies a more humane approach, letting students live together as a unit and attend the same classes. For the most part, classes are less formally structured, and students can select the instructors for some required subjects. One course, LAS 110, is used by volunteer faculty to offer a variety of courses, either to individuals or small groups studying a subject of mutual interest not ordinarily available. Those involved in the program cite its feeling of close community as one advantage.

A second consequence of the new openness in higher learning is a loosening of traditional requirements for college entrance.

With so much in flux on the campus itself, it is becoming increasingly absurd for colleges to insist that applicants meet a rigid, arbitrary set of requirements for entrance. College admissions people are well aware of this. Yet many conscientious secondary school people still believe that permitting the flexibility that would obviously be beneficial in junior and senior year programs would damage the best students' chances of getting into the colleges of their choice. Now there is less reason for fearfulness.

A third important implication of changes in higher learning is that the lockstep, uninterrupted march through sixteen or more years of schooling may finally be breaking. So many students are electing to "stop out" for a year or two before moving from high school to college that many of the leading colleges are now making explicit and nonpunitive arrangements for a delay in entering. Again, this new flexibility should be a boon for all concerned. A greater interpenetration of school and the "real world" is healthful. By overcoming any existing prejudice against students who don't come directly from high school, colleges are leaving the door to higher learning open for more people all the time.

A fourth immediate consequence is a change in today's students. A well-noted current social phenomenon is that parents are resuming their own formal education, especially young and middle-aged mothers who had to curtail their education before or during college. And colleges, having begun to run out of young people to teach, are making these older students' migration back to campus as easy and pleasant as possible. Far from the disdain and discomfort that used to greet them in the classroom, adult students are now not only welcomed when they come but also actively sought after by colleges. Special weekend, evening, and personalized courses of study are provided for them, and they are often helped to obtain academic credit for their life learning, as we have seen.

The point is that many of these students are parents of children now in school. Recent findings have revealed that in many cases the parents' involvement in education has a significant positive effect on the children, who are motivated, excited, stimulated, and supported by awareness that their parents take education seriously and are themselves studying, reading, writing, and going to classes. So the opening of higher education, involving many adults, is having an important effect right now on the character of many youngsters in school.

A further extension of this effect may be predicted, though here we enter the realm of the cloudy crystal ball. It is not entirely fanciful to anticipate that college graduates who have gone through a culminating educational experience that is individualized, flexible, relevant, and largely self-determined may want similar opportunities for their children from the earliest grades. Certainly teachers know from their experiences in working with parents that the parent's image of learning and teaching comes from his or her own schooling. They also know that one of the toughest problems in introducing innovation is convincing parents that a style of education different from the one they experienced can be better and more effective. So opening higher learning may be an important consciousness-raiser for the next generation of parents.

Perhaps the most profound implication of open education for schools is a theoretical one concerning the curriculum. Reforms in higher education mean that learning is coming to be conceived of as a lifelong process rather than one confined to the years of formal schooling. The whole higher education establishment is going through an agonizing shift, recognizing that in the future it must serve not only the 18- to 22-year-olds but also people of all ages who want and need to learn. There is serious talk of educational sabbaticals for many kinds of workers, of mandatory retraining of professionals to assure that they keep up with burgeoning knowledge in their fields, of "entitlements" that would permit adults to decide when and how they would regularly acquire more education.

As this trend toward lifelong learning grows, it will make our present conception of school curriculum obsolete. The "front-end-load" theory, that we need to give the student in the time spent in school what is needed for the rest of life, has been recognized as fallacious by vanguard educators for some time. "Learning *how to learn*" has been recognized for decades as the proper function of schooling. But that insight will be reenforced, strengthened, and greatly amplified when people at any stage of life can and do return to learning as a practical matter. Moreover, an edge will be added to the tenet as it becomes apparent that not even the

American economy can afford both a full-fledged system of lifelong learning and a system of schooling as richly financed as ours still is. Some real confrontations within society over allocation of funds for education of all kinds may soon appear.

Those who advocate more and better "front-end" schooling will confront those who want to strengthen lifelong learning. Such a struggle can already be witnessed in some communities over federal funds provided by the Comprehensive Employment and Training Act. These funds can be used by a wide variety of individuals, depending on who has the initiative to set up appropriate programs or the clout to have a program given preference. In some communities groups who believe the funds should be used for youngsters are fighting against those who think they should be available to mid-career adults. Such struggles may become commonplace in the near future.

Finally, some less tangible and more long-range effects may be important. The educational values of the academy have always exerted a considerable influence on schools. The campus ideal of what is worth learning and how it can best be taught has always provided a powerful example for the rest of education. That is why high schools have modeled their curriculum and teaching styles after those of colleges and failed for so long to find pedagogical formats truly appropriate for adolescent youngsters.

One reason is that teachers in the schools teach not so much the way they were taught to teach as the way they were taught. Especially in secondary education, teachers model themselves on professors they admired in college rather than on theories they were taught in their methods courses.

As the style of pedagogy in higher learning changes, therefore, we may expect a profound effect on teaching styles of the next generation of teachers. Learning from professors who function not merely as conveyors of knowledge and authorities in their fields, but also as mentors, guides, facilitators, and learning consultants, college students of the seventies, who will be the young teachers of the eighties, will imbibe a different sense of what it means to help students to learn.

SELECTED BIBLIOGRAPHY

Blaze, Wayne, et. al., *Guide to Alternative Colleges and Universities*, Boston: Beacon, 1974. A listing of more than 250 programs, mostly campus-based B.A. programs but also including two-year A.A. programs, external degrees, and free universities. The annotations are engagingly personal and opinionated.

Commission on Nontraditional Study, *Diversity by Design*, San Francisco: Jossey-Bass, 1973. The milestone book in this field, proposing the priorities, styles, and specific practices that the Commission concluded would enable higher education to meet new social needs.

Coyne, John, and Hebert, Tom, *This Way Out: A Guide to Alternatives to Traditional College Education*, New York: Dutton, 1972. A directory, like the Guide above, but focused on experimental colleges and also covering study opportunities in Europe and the Third World. The entries are full, informal, and pointed. A 100-page guide to independent study, based on the proposition, "You don't need a college to get a higher education any more," is brash but stimulating.

Eis, Jennifer, and Ward, Don, *Taking Off: An Organizational Handbook and Comprehensive Worldwide Resource Guide for Nontraditional Higher Education*, East Lansing: Center for Alternatives in/to Higher Education, Michigan State University, 1975. A compilation of "organizations that place students in a great variety of learning situations" grouped under such functional categories as "Outdoor Living," "Performing Arts," "Science and Technology." Prefaced with a substantial handbook on how to create such learning environments.

Gross, Ronald, and Gross, Beatrice, eds., *Will It Grow in a Classroom?*, New York: Delacorte, 1974. Teacher-to-teacher communications about successful ways to enhance learning in elementary and secondary classrooms.

Gross, Ronald, and Osterman, Paul, eds., *High School*, New York: Simon and Schuster, 1973. Theoretical papers and case studies advocating openness in secondary education.

Hall, Laurence, and associates, *New Colleges for New Students*, San Francisco: Jossey-Bass, 1974. Well written (by leading educational journalists) case studies of outstanding nontraditional programs serving previously bypassed students in innovative ways.

Levine, Arthur, and Weingart, John, *Reform of Undergraduate Education,* San Francisco: Jossey-Bass, 1973. A critical analysis of some of the most popular innovations in higher learning, based on study and interviews on twenty-six campuses.

Taylor, Harold, *How to Change the Colleges,* New York: Holt, Rinehart and Winston, 1971. The best treatment of the subject by the most humane voice in higher education criticism.

Vermilye, Dyckman W., ed., *Lifelong Learners—A New Clientele for Higher Education,* San Francisco: Jossey-Bass, 1974. Papers ranging from theoretical discussions of "Education, Work, and Quality of Life" to "Writing a Learning Contract," drawn from the 1974 annual conference of the American Association for Higher Education.

Two good sources of information about innovative programs in higher education are: Office of New Degree Programs, College Entrance Examination Board, 888 Seventh Avenue, New York, NY 10019 (John Valley, director); and NEXUS, c/o American Association for Higher Education, One Dupont Circle, Washington, D.C. 20036 (Jane Lichtman, director).

```
LB 2341 .G75

Gross, Ronald.

Diversity in higher
 education :
                    325409
```

**UNIVERSITY OF WISCONSIN
LIBRARY**
Stevens Point, Wisconsin

This book and others in the series are made available at low cost through the contribution of the Phi Delta Kappa Educational Foundation, established in 1966 with a bequest by George H. Reavis. The Foundation exists to promote a better understanding of the nature of the educative process and the relation of education to human welfare. It operates by subsidizing authors to write booklets and monographs in nontechnical language so that beginning teachers and the public generally may gain a better understanding of educational problems.

The Foundation exists through the generosity of George Reavis and others who have contributed. To accomplish the goals envisaged by the founder the Foundation needs to enlarge its endowment by several million dollars. Contributions to the endowment should be addressed to The Educational Foundation, Phi Delta Kappa, 8th and Union, Bloomington, Indiana 47401. The Ohio State University serves as trustee for the Educational Foundation.

You, the reader, can contribute to the improvement of educational literature by reporting your reactions to this fastback. What is the outstanding strength of this publication? The glaring weakness? What topics do you suggest for future fastbacks? Write to Director of Special Publications, PHI DELTA KAPPA, Eighth and Union, Box 789, Bloomington, IN 47401.

All seventy-eight titles can be purchased for $23.00 ($19.00 for paid-up members of Phi Delta Kappa).

Any six titles $3.00 (only $2.00 for members); twelve titles $5.00 (only $4.00 for members).

Discounts for bulk orders of the same title are allowed at the rate of 10 to 25, 10%; 26 to 99, 20%; 100 to 499, 30%; 500 to 999, 40%; 1000 or more 50%. Discounts are based on a unit cost of 50¢ per copy (35¢ for members).

MONEY MUST ACCOMPANY ALL ORDERS FOR LESS THAN $5.00 OR ADD $1.00 FOR HANDLING.

Order from: PHI DELTA KAPPA, Eighth and Union, Box 789, Bloomington, Indiana 47401